THE
JOY
OF USHERS AND HOSPITALITY MINISTERS

Making a Place for Others

Gretchen Hailer, RSHM

*For my mother and father,
Grace Sheerin Hailer and Joseph Allen Hailer,
from whom I first learned a sense of hospitality. I
know they now share the hospitality of
the **Wilcum** in their heavenly home.*

First published in September, 2000 by Resurrection Press, Catholic Book Publishing Company.

Copyright © 2000 by Gretchen Hailer, RSHM

ISBN 1-878718-60-6

Library of Congress Catalog Number 133392

All rights reserved. No part of this book may be reproduced or transmitted in any form or by any means, electronic or mechanical, including photocopying, recording, or by any information storage and retrieval system without permission in writing from the publisher.

Cover design by John Murello

Printed in the United States of America.

2 3 4 5 6 7 8 9

The Joy of Ushers and Hospitality Ministers
Making a Place for Others

Contents

Acknowledgement   7

Introduction   8

Foreword   10

Chapter 1
    A Place of Welcome   13

Chapter 2
    A Place of Comfort   19

Chapter 3
    A Place of Respect   25

Chapter 4
    A Place of Participation   31

Chapter 5
    A Place of Safety   37

Chapter 6
    A Place of Belonging   43

Chapter 7
    A Place of Thanksgiving   49

Chapter 8
    A Place of Affirmation   55

Acknowledgement

A special thanks to all the hospitality ministers in scores of parishes who have graciously shared their stories with me over the last few months. These stories, some funny, some poignant, some downright edifying, attest to the wonderful sense of service these pastoral ministers provide for their sisters and brothers.

Introduction

SO, how long have you been an usher? Twenty years, really? That's great!

And you, how long have you been in the church hospitality business? Just started? Good for you!

Well, regardless of whether you're an old timer at church hospitality or just a beginner, this little booklet is for you. It represents a lot of experience from ushers and hospitality ministers all over North America—and beyond. Hopefully, much of what it has to offer is already happening in your parish. As you read over the contents, imagine how you and/or your hospitality team can incorporate its best ideas into your strategy of welcome.

As you can see, the structure of this resource makes it quite easy to use:

- √ Opening Psalm passage
- √ Usher story
- √ Reflection material
- √ Group reflection questions
- √ Personal response
- √ Closing prayer

Because of its division into six short content chapters and two resource chapters, the material can really be used in six separate gatherings of a diocesan or deanery training program. Or the material might be better presented as helpful content for a one day retreat held in the parish just before the "regular" pace resumes in the fall. The ideal retreat day would be held on a Saturday, ending with the parish vigil Mass where hospitality ministers could be installed for service to that local community. A festive dinner could follow the Eucharist.

Whatever way the material in this little booklet is used, it is hoped that what is written here might be just the thing to help you better understand the gift that you are asked to share with your local church community.

Hopefully you, too, will appreciate the joy of helping other believers find their place!

Enjoy and God bless you in your special ministry.

Foreword

THE English word *usher* shares the same root as the French *(h)uissier*. An *huissier* is an officer of the peace or an officer of justice. That seems a fitting title for someone whose job it is to model the welcome we received at baptism, as Sr. Gretchen Hailer points out in these eight chapters. It is a welcome into a new order and a new way of being. It is a welcome into a place where the blind see, the lame walk, and the deaf hear.

We also call these servants of the church "hospitality ministers." The connection with "hospital" is also apt for those who comfort and offer safekeeping and belonging to those who approach our open doors.

These keepers of our doors have a responsibility much more vast than finding empty seats for late comers and passing envelope baskets. They are the initial face of Christ for the seekers and saints who gather for worship. They are the first real presence of the community we encounter. They are our living worship aids as they assure our temporal needs are met, freeing us to focus on the work—the liturgy—we have gathered to do.

This ministry, if taken seriously, requires commitment. Through our baptism we are called to put the needs of others before our own. Ushers and hospitality ministers are particularly called to show that kind of concern. If we take hospitality to the extreme, as Jesus did, that could mean putting the life of another before our own. Such an ultimate sacrifice is not required of most of us. But all of us promise to offer it, if necessary, every time we gather for worship. And our "peace officers" are special examples of that promise.

We hope that many of the ideas presented here will not come as new information to most ushers and hospitality ministers. But the stories and gentle urgings to be more like Christ will inspire even the most accomplished minister to a deeper level of commitment—to the community, to justice, and the building up of God's kingdom.

Nick Wagner

— One —

A PLACE OF WELCOME

Psalm Passage

"I would rather be a doorkeeper in the house of my God, than to dwell in the tents of the wicked."
(Ps 84:11)

Usher Story

I remember the time our pastor had a friend of his dress up like a street person to see how welcoming we were. We all failed miserably: from greeters, to ushers, to congregation. We booted the poor guy out, is what we did!

And then to make matters worse, the pastor had already arranged that the fellow would come down the aisle at the Presentation of the Gifts–alone–with the bread and wine and his head held high. When he went right up and stood next to Father at the altar and both smiled at us, we got their meaning, let me tell you!"

Allan—Chicago, Illinois

Reflection

Welcome and hospitality are part and parcel of our Christian life. The greatest welcome we ever received was at the baptismal font where we were immersed in the very life of God. Jesus said, "Whoever welcomes you welcomes me, and whoever welcomes me welcomes the One who sent me" (Mt. 10:40).

In fact, our present English word, welcome, derives from the word, *Wilcum,* which means, "Desired Guest." This was the person, in days gone by, who arrived at your door, most often unannounced. In that hospitable culture, the expectation was on the doorkeeper to greet the person and accompany them into the master's presence. The householder and his family, in their turn, offered the guest words of welcome and news, food and drink, and a place of rest. The next day, the *Wilcum* was accompanied to the door and sent on his or her way with a well meant, "Godspeed!"

When you come to think of it, your role as greeter or usher is much like that early doorkeeper. Your ministry on behalf of the local family of believers is to welcome those–parishioners and strangers alike–who appear at the door of the church. You, indeed, accompany them into

A Place of Welcome 15

the Master's presence where we present day followers share the Good News and break the Bread of the Eucharist.

Please note that as official welcomer, the initial greeting that you extend at the door, in the vestibule or aisle, needn't be extensive. Actually, it should not be drawn out. A simple, "Hello," "Welcome folks," or "Glad to see you again," is ample. Adding the person's name provides a wonderful personal touch. And remember, in the case of names that are a bit tricky to pronounce, call the person by the name they use. If she says her name is Graciela, then don't call her Gracie!

Without doubt, the last piece of a complete welcome to each parishioner is the gift of your smile. Yes, a good ol' smile and personal greeting can literally make someone's day!

The Hospitality Team

So, who are these generous folks who make up today's parish doorkeepers? Well, since they are called to represent the entire community, they should reflect the make-up of all the parishioners. By that we mean that greeters and ushers should come in both genders, embody all ages, and comprise the variety of cultures and languages that make up the local parish.

Sometimes this "team" is difficult to assemble. In not a few parishes, a small but mighty group has been ushering for years! These capable people should be encouraged to continue their service, but NEVER to the exclusion of others who desire to join in this important ministry.

Now, while genuine welcome is an essential responsibility of the parish doorkeepers, it is really only a minor part of their work of service. It is actually the entire parish assembly who is called to inclusive hospitality. Each one who makes up the worshiping community ought to welcome others and each other as a *Wilcum*, or "Desired Guest."

A Place of Welcome 17

Group Reflection Questions

1. In what way do the greeters and ushers in your parish work together to insure that people are treated as "Desired Guest?" Who among your parish hospitality colleagues do you consider especially good at what they do? Why?

2. How do you all ensure that people know who you are and where and when they can expect to find you at your post?

3. Are hospitality ministers and ushers available for other functions besides Sunday Eucharist in your parish community? What are these functions? Or what could these functions be?

Personal Response

1. What are the most satisfying thoughts or feelings that you have when you think of yourself as a minister of welcome?

2. What are the most challenging?

Prayer

Loving God, gracious host, help me/us to see each person who approaches the doors of our parish church as a "Desired Guest," your desired guest. May I/we always try to reach out to others as you would. Help me/us to deepen my/our understanding that I/we serve as your minister(s) of welcome.

AMEN.

— Two —

A PLACE OF COMFORT

Psalm Passage

"Pleasant places have been marked out for me by the measuring lines. Delightful indeed is my inheritance." (Ps 16:6)

Usher Story

IT was right at the start of Desert Storm and my husband had just shipped out. There I was at a 9:30 Mass, alone with 9 month old Abbie, 3 year old Joey, and 5 year old Jackie. As you can imagine I was a bit rattled and flustered.

Then from nowhere came this knight in shining armor. He saluted me, said, "Hang in there, ma'am" and then handed me two baggies of Cheerios for the older kids. I found out later that Usher Nick was a Vietnam vet and well loved by the kids and hassled parents of our parish community. *Millie—Pensacola, Florida*

Reflection

Comfort is a somewhat relative term, isn't it? It can connote a number of things: from physical well-being to solace or even encouragement. Of course for you as usher or hospitality minister it will, at one time or another, mean all of the above.

Helping to create a place of comfort for your fellow parishioners is really about noticing. And noticing in the presence of a crowd of several hundred people is anything but easy. However with a few agreed upon ground rules, the hospitality team can really create a comforting place for worshipers which can provide physical well-being as well as encouragement.

Be Prepared

First of all, upon your timely arrival, check out the surroundings from front (and side) door, through the vestibule and main body of the church, to the sanctuary area to make sure the temperature inside is well within a comfortable zone. If windows need to be opened or closed, or thermostat adjusted, that should be done well before folks arrive. In your sweep through the main body of the building, collect any stray articles that need to be brought to the place where lost and found items are stored. And even though, most certainly, the parish has a custodian, he or she possibly doesn't work on the weekends. So check to see that restrooms are open and stocked with necessary paper supplies.

If your church has some sort of storage area for coats and boots, make certain that it is accessible and that hangers are available. There's nothing more uncomfortable than having to wear a soggy jacket or wet boots during Mass.

Finding a Place

One of the main things ushers do for the community, of course, is to help worshipers find seats. This may sound easier said than done. While most ushers already know by instinct that stuffing pews like sardine cans is not the most gracious act of hospitality, there still is the reality of finding folks places to sit. Here, simply noticing is a big help. If there is a large gap in any one pew and there are people in need of a place, suggest to the occupants, *with a smile*, that they provide space. Or if you happen to see among the stand-up worshipers, a person who probably needs a sit-down spot, approach some strong looking person and ask for their help in providing a place. As always, a generous amount of tact is also in order, especially on big occasions when the worshipers number more than usual.

Special Needs

Keep your eyes out for people with special needs. These folks call for various kinds of personal attention. Imagine what these needs might be and then ask the person (or their caretaker) how you can make things easier for them to celebrate the Eucharist fully. Once you come up with a creative response, make sure you share it with other team members. In some cases, as with the physically challenged, there needs to be both a plan and a place for them. This may require suggesting that a front pew be removed so that wheel chairs (or even folks with walkers) will have spots close to the sanctuary. Or you and your team members may need to provide personal amplifiers for the hearing impaired. It's not unheard of that in the summer a faithful seeing eye dog might well be thirsty and merit a well-earned drink of water!

Group Reflection Questions

1. What is your attitude toward "straightening up" the church environment before and after Mass? Do you find yourself saying, "It's not my job!" or do you really embrace your responsibility to create a place of comfort for others?

2. In what way does your hospitality team have a place and a plan for parishioners with special needs?

3. What other considerations for the comfort of worshipers can you think of that have not been included here?

Personal Response

1. What are the most satisfying thoughts or feelings that you have when you think of yourself as a provider of comfort?

2. What are the most challenging?

Prayer

Spirit of God, "Comforter," come to my/our assistance. Be my/our vision; help me/us notice the needs of others before they even ask for help. Strengthen me/us to respond in love and kindness to all who need a provider of comfort during our time of worship.

AMEN.

— Three —

A PLACE OF RESPECT

Psalm Passage

"Praise the Lord, all you nations; extol God all you peoples. How great is God's love for us!"
(Ps 117:1)

Usher Story

ONE of the first times I came to Mass here in America, I was shocked when one of the men of the parish, standing in the center aisle, motioned to me as if offering me a place to sit, BUT using a hand gesture that in my culture is one of great disrespect!

I was confused and sad. After church, I told our elder about the insult and he said, "The man thinks he is helping, not hurting. Perhaps, though, it would be good if I went and told him what the gesture means to us in our culture."

The next week, when we arrived, the usher came and said how sorry he was to have offended us by his ignorance. I am happy now for his act of respect and friendship.

Haet—Stockton, California

Reflection

Culture and respect should go hand in hand. Unfortunately, many of the stories we read in the newspaper or see on the evening news don't bear that out. Often we learn there that because of some misunderstanding or worse—a refusal to understand—a terrible rupture in neighborhood relations is experienced somewhere.

It doesn't take too much reflection on the name "Catholic" to know that our Christian heritage embraces the whole world. In real life, this means that Jesus the Christ is known, respected and loved in thousands of cultures.

So what is culture? And why talk about culture anyway? Well, we know that it's not an easy thing to define, but it involves all the shared attitudes, values, behaviors, and institutions of a particular society. It can be uncovered in the stories, jokes, language and gestures of a group. Indeed, culture is the way that people make sense out of their world.

And let's be honest: North America is becoming more multi-cultural than it has ever been. This means that our community of believers reflects this reality as well. Be assured that respect for the myriad ways that ethnic and other groups express themselves during worship is a must if we are to become truly "Catholic."

Correct Gestures

Just as our usher story intimated, certain gestures or facial expressions we take for granted are foreign to the culture of others. And the flip side of that reality is also true: we can't assume to know what folks of another culture really mean by something they might say or do. During the Rite of Peace, for example, it is a simple thing to accept a bow from an Asian member of our community rather than expect a vigorous handshake. And our Asian sisters and brothers will appreciate our openness to accept their greeting with a gesture that is familiar to them.

Adolescents are well worth a mention here when we speak of cultures. They, as all age groups, have a special culture that marks them. Many times, as adults, we find their "ways" foreign to us and tend not to reach out to them.

When we are fortunate as a parish to have our young people choose to be among us, we should surely treat them as "Desired Guest." In fact, our respect for them is further reflected when we include youth as members of our hospitality team.

Difficult Situations

There will be times as ushers and greeters that we will have to deal with people whose behavior in church is not itself respectful of other worshipers. When this happens, as in the case of late arrivals, intoxicated Midnight Mass attendees, cell phone users, or parents of crying or disruptive children, the place and plan concept can really come in handy. Treat each case individually, discreetly, and politely, but having already prepared for such eventualities.

Late arrivals who want to walk to their place during the Liturgy of the Word, should be requested not to do so as the Word is proclaimed by lector, deacon, or presider. Or ushers may want to reserve the back pews for late comers. Holiday revelers should be reminded gently that they are now in church, with others who are trying to engage in holy day worship.

Church should certainly be a cell phone free zone. A simple sign in the vestibule should be sufficient to remind users that the device should be turned off. Parents with children whose cranky behavior has produced annoyed stares and less than silent "shhs" from those around them, need to be encouraged to return to their seat once the child is doing a bit better!

When all is said and done, these messages of respect lead to the kind of communal reverence that contributes to good liturgy; the kind of reverence that reflects the fact that we believe that this is God's house and we are happy, as God's people, to worship here together.

Group Reflection Questions

1. How have you become aware of the various cultures that make up your parish community? Have you ever thought of offering a greeting to others in their native language? Why or why not?

2. What are some problematic situations that you have experienced as a hospitality minister that

have caused you concern. What did you find yourself doing to respond? Would you still respond the same way? Why or why not?

3. When you have attended Mass in a foreign country or parish with a culture quite different from your own, what did you notice most about the ways people reached out (or not!) to you? How can you incorporate a similar respectful outreach in your home parish?

Personal Response

1. What are the most satisfying thoughts or feelings that you have when you think of yourself as a messenger of respect?

2. What are the most challenging?

Prayer

Creator God, you delight in the diversity of the people you have made. I/we give thanks for the many faces and languages and cultures that make up my/our parish community. May I/we always be a messenger of respect for them in my/our manner of service.

AMEN.

— Four —

A PLACE OF PARTICIPATION

Psalm Passage

"How can I repay the Lord for all his goodness to me? I will lift up the cup of salvation and call on the name of the Lord." (Ps 116:12-13)

Usher Story

WELL, she was the cutest thing, a little tyke in a pretty dress, sitting with her family at Mass. I smiled at her each time I passed their pew, and at one point noticed that she was holding a shiny quarter in her chubby hand. I figured she anticipated her part in the collection in a big way.

At the preparation time as the gifts were gathered for presentation, I approached her pew and she readily dropped her money in the basket. You can imagine my surprise, then, when a few benches beyond hers, I heard, "Hey, lady! I want my money back. Give me back my quarter!"

Bea—Butte, Montana

Reflection

Naturally, the Eucharist is about participation. As Vatican II reminds us, it is the sign and source of our unity. Participation is about the parts becoming a whole. The more participation, the more deeply we can experience that unity among us.

The hospitality ministers, as facilitators of participation, should be the first to model it for their sisters and brothers in the assembly. Having ushers who stand in twos around the back of the church talking together simply does not mirror participation! That's why, in many parishes, ushers sit with their families once Mass has begun and stay there during the Liturgy of the Word.

Anticipating Needs

As facilitators of participation, ushers and greeters need to be anticipators as well. That means finding out ahead of time what special things might be needed during any one particular liturgy. If there is to be a special collection, the envelopes have to be available whether in racks in the pews, stacked neatly at the end of each aisle or, in hand, ready to be passed out at the designated

A Place of Participation

time. If some sort of diocesan or parish survey is being conducted, then those handouts (and pencils, too) have to be ready. The presider or others should not have to request the cooperation of the ushers, you should be alert and prepared.

If your liturgy committee encourages the use of hymn books or worship aids, these should be passed out as people enter the church or pointed out to worshipers in the pews. Here's one area where hospitality ministers clearly can be models of participation. There is no reason why members of the team should be cruising the aisles once Mass has begun. In fact, ushers then become just as distracting as late arrivals. If you are seen singing and joining in acclamations and other responses, then the other members of the congregation will be encouraged to do the same.

Facilitating Processions

As to times during the Eucharist when movement is part of the activity of the people, ushers should be available to help with the processions. At the beginning of Mass, hospitality ministers need to be of assistance so that the Entrance Procession can make its way through the assembly to the sanctuary. Again at the time of the

Presentation of the Gifts, and before they themselves take up the collection, ushers might be called upon to gather those already chosen to bring up the gifts. Depending on custom, an usher often brings up a basket with the collection money after the bread and wine have been brought to the altar. The basket with our monetary gifts, however, should never be placed directly on the altar.

It is worth mentioning here that processions are not just about getting people or things from one place to another. In our Christian worship, processions have a highly symbolic purpose and that is to remind us that we, as a community, are on our way to God's Kingdom.

The Communion Procession is another time where the assembly moves from one place to another. At this point, be attentive to those who may wish (or need) to have communion brought to them at their place. Usually Eucharistic Ministers make provision for this kindness, but often wait until the rest of the community has received communion. Keep an eye out, then, in case they forget.

At the close of the Liturgy, it is a good thing if you position yourself in such a way as to provide an easy exit for the ministers who are processing from the sanctuary to the back of the church. If, later, there should be a bottleneck caused by folks blocking the aisles as they chat with one another, you might want to suggest politely that they continue their conversation in the pews or outside the church building.

So you see, as facilitator of participation you have a lot to attend to during Mass, but you will be rewarded by the unity you have encouraged.

Group Reflection Questions

1. What is your understanding of your role to model participation yourself?

2. Does your hospitality team have a clear understanding of how and where various processions during Mass begin, proceed, and end? Do you have a place and plan for these movements?

3. Is there someone on the team charged with finding out ahead of time what might be taking place within the Liturgy that calls for special readiness on the part of ushers and

greeters? Who is that? How are these needs then communicated to the team?

Personal Response

1. What are the most satisfying thoughts or feelings that you have when you think of yourself as a facilitator of participation?
2. What are the most challenging?

Prayer

Jesus, you who said, "wherever two or three are gathered in my name, there I am in their midst," help me/us to be alert and prepared during the Mass to be a real facilitator of participation, never a hindrance.

AMEN.

— Five —

A PLACE OF SAFETY

❧

Psalm Passage

"The Lord will guard you from evil; the Lord will protect your life. The Lord will watch over your coming and going both now and forever."

(Ps 121:7-8)

Usher Story

HERE'S the truth: a man came into our inner city parish just before Eucharist began and fell to the floor in the back of the church. He was bleeding and it didn't take much to note that he had been shot!

While one of the ushers ran over to comfort the victim, the priest began to pray aloud with the congregation for the man and the safety of all the assembly. A greeter called 911 and a nurse who usually attends that Mass came quickly to the man's side to administer first aid.

After the paramedics sped off with the injured man, one of the parishioners said aloud, "Now we can continue with the liturgy because we have truly found the suffering Jesus in our midst.

(Some weeks later, we received a note from the man and his family, thanking us for our quick response to his need.)

Therese—Baltimore, Maryland

Reflection

Many of us take it for granted that our time spent in church at worship will be a time of physical and emotional security. This is not always the case and the members of the parish hospitality team need to be prepared for emergencies, great and small.

Once again, anticipating needs in advance is the most prudent strategy and most ushers know the importance of having an emergency plan, with everyone on the hospitality team and liturgy committee knowing their specific role in the safety effort. It is important that the newer members of the team be shown all exits, quickest evacuation routes, as well as the location of fire extinguishers and how to use them.

Most dioceses have a crisis or disaster plan for their particular part of the country. As we well

A Place of Safety

know, each region has natural disasters that can visit us with very little notice. Earthquakes, tornadoes and other dramatic phenomena of nature come to mind, but there is also the need to be alert for fire, power outages, wet floors, broken kneelers, or even falling ceiling tiles.

A combination of calm and competence is the appropriate response in any emergency; but even the best of us can become rattled under trying circumstances. So training is in order for the hospitality team. At least one person at each Mass should have training in first aid and CPR (cardiopulmonary resuscitation). In addition, each usher and greeter has to know where the emergency first aid kit is, what is in it, and when it is appropriate to use what is inside. Parishioners who are health professionals can be of assistance here and even provide the training for your team, if asked. The fact that you know who these important people are (and what Mass they generally attend) will extend your first aid outreach.

When someone is taken ill during the Eucharist, try to assist them with the least amount of fuss possible. This saves them possible embarrassment and creates the calm that is needed for their well-being.

The Collection

Another safety consideration should be mentioned: that is, the way in which the collection is taken up and taken care of afterwards. This may sound obvious, but many hospitality ministers approach their role only in its many parts rather than having a complete overview.

In the case of watching the collection while it is being taken up, it is just prudent to keep an eye on whatever type of basket or other container you use to gather the monetary gifts of the assembly. Often the hospitality team captain (or whatever title your parish gives him or her) is the ultimate one responsible for the collection once it is carried up to the sanctuary. This usually means taking the money to the sacristy or other secure place.

Keeping Them Safe and Secure

Another thing to be mindful of is that many women parishioners leave their handbags in the pews when they join the Communion Procession. As has been mentioned before, noticing is the order of the day with all security concerns.

A final safety reminder has to do with evening Masses and making certain that solitary worshipers, especially the frail elderly, are offered the possibility of accompaniment to the parking lot or front of the church to await busses or taxis. Common sense is the rule here, particularly if the parking lot is not well lighted or your parish is located in a non-residential area.

Generally, if these suggestions regarding safety are discussed with the group, your parish security plan will be fleshed out more concretely and each member of the hospitality team will know his or her role.

❦

Group Reflection Questions

1. In what ways do you function best in an emergency situation? Do you know how your other team members respond? Why is it important to know?

2. Does your diocese and/or local parish have a crisis or disaster plan? In what does it consist?

3. What type of emergency have you already experienced in your role as usher or greeter? What do you think could have been done differently to insure a better outcome?

Personal Reflection

1. What are the most satisfying thoughts or feelings that you have when you think of yourself as an agent of safety?

2. What are the most challenging?

Prayer

God of peace, be with me/us as I/we try to create a haven of safety in our place of worship. Keep me/us competent and calm as I/we provide for the emergency needs of our congregation. Be with us always.

AMEN.

— Six —

A PLACE OF BELONGING

Psalm Passage

"For the sake of my relatives and friends I will say, 'Peace be with you!' For the sake of the house of our Lord, I will pray for your good."

(Ps 122:8-9)

Usher Story

SO Maria, one of our greeters at Mass, says to me, "Carlos, check out this announcement in the bulletin. We could use someone creative like you at the festival committee meeting this Thursday."

I told her that I was no good in groups, but come Thursday my wife said, "Honey, give it a try. You'll be good."

Well, I did give it a try and I was good and so was the festival! And I'm happy that someone thought to invite me into the group.

Carlos—Albuquerque, New Mexico

Reflection

Just as hospitality ministers begin their service by helping fellow worshipers feel welcome in the community, so too they end their Mass assignment with the hopes that everyone who attended the Eucharist on their watch felt a real sense of belonging, a real sense of being a "Desired Guest."

Generally, the final responsibility of the ushers and greeters is to reverse the welcoming actions that they used to meet people before Mass began. The one additional task, of course, after helping to collect hymn books and worship aids is to distribute the parish bulletins and other handouts.

Many parishes choose to keep the parish bulletins out of sight at the beginning of Mass. The reason is simple: by not having the bulletins available at the doors when people enter, they are more apt to listen to the proclamation of the Word and the reflection of the homilist.

There is also something more personal about receiving a parish bulletin as one leaves the church. And, as is noted in the anecdote at the beginning of this chapter, really observant hospitality ministers have gotten to know the folks who come to worship at their parish each week. If that sense of relationship has developed, then it follows naturally that you will be able to make connections between volunteer requests and meeting days and times with the gifts or interests of various members of the congregation. Of course, this means that you are diligent in reading over the contents of the bulletin beforehand.

Scheduling the Team

A word about providing a sense of continuity in your place of belonging. What is meant here is that most folks feel more at home the more familiar they are with a place and the people there. It might be a good thing, if you have not already discussed it among yourselves, to decide if at your parish there is more value in keeping the schedules of the hospitality team constant or in varying them. There are good points in favor of each approach.

If people know that YOU will always be at the 11:00 Mass, they will feel immediately at home when they spot your smiling face. Consistent presence allows relationships to develop. On the other hand, something can be said for the fact that varying time schedules helps both ushers and greeters as well as worshipers from getting in a rut.

Whatever your parish chooses to do about scheduling hospitality team members, please be there–on time and smiling–so that everyone will feel a real sense of community and belonging.

Educating the Community

Finally, it might be helpful that the role of ushers (and other ministers) is explained to the congregation periodically. This can be done verbally by the hospitality team leader or various members at all the Masses or simply written up in the parish bulletin. This acknowledges the service that both ushers and greeters provide as well as encourages support of your various procedures among the parishioners. It will also educate the community as to the many ministries that take place in their parish.

Group Reflection Questions

1. What is your plan for the distribution of parish bulletins and other materials? Are they put out before Mass or kept out of sight until after Mass? Why? Or why not?

2. How do you feel about the Mass schedules for ushers and greeters? Do you think consistency or variety of scheduling is best? Why? Or why not?

3. Have you tried to establish relationships with fellow parishioners so that they know that you care about them? How have you done this?

Personal Reflection

1. What are the most satisfying thoughts or feelings that you have when you think of yourself as a community animator?

2. What are the most challenging?

Prayer

Holy Trinity, one God, thank you for modeling for me/us a sense of community and belonging. May my/our thoughtful actions help animate others in such a way that they bring the Sunday Eucharist into their daily lives and the lives of those around them.

AMEN.

— Seven —

A PLACE OF THANKSGIVING

Psalm Passage

"You are my God, and I give you thanks. You are my God, and I give you praise. Give thanks to the Lord, who is good; whose steadfast love endures forever!" (Ps 118:28-29)

Usher Story

MOM and Dad were greeters and ushers for as long as the Church had encouraged lay people to be involved in parish ministries. Each of them had the special gift that it takes to make people feel welcome and part of the community at Mass. It always made me proud to see them at the doors of the church and then, again, helping everything run smoothly during the Eucharist.

When Mom died, my Dad was crushed. But when we arrived at church for her Mass of Christian Burial, a huge smile spread across my father's face. Word had gotten around that Mom had died, and there in front of the building were scores of parishioners with signs saying things like, "May the angels welcome YOU to paradise," and, "May the saints guard you on your way."

Pat—St. Paul, Minnesota

Reflection

As you know, the word Eucharist means "thanksgiving." It celebrates the great act of Christian thanks to God for the gift of Jesus. With so wonderful an act on the part of God, then, how much gratitude should be yours in the ministry of helping others find their special place at Eucharist.

It stands to reason that, with such a noble service to be rendered to your sisters and brothers, you take seriously your obligation to fully understand your role in this communal act of thanksgiving.

With this in mind, take some time to review the various parts of the Mass outlined here and the important part you play during them.

A Place of Thanksgiving

Order of Mass

Introductory Rites

Gathering Song and Procession

Presider's Greeting

Kyrie (Lord/Christ have mercy)

Gloria (Glory to God in the highest)

Opening Prayer

[What's going on here is that those who have arrived for Mass are being gathered together into a worshiping community; your job is to help facilitate this transformation.]

Liturgy of the Word

First Reading

Psalm Response

Second Reading

Gospel Acclamation/Proclamation

Homily

Profession of Faith (Creed)

General Intercessions

[What's happening now is that the inspired Word from the Hebrew and Christian Scriptures is read, responded to, commented on, and prayed about; your role is to help create a quiet, listening environment.]

Liturgy of the Eucharist (Preparation)

Preparation of the Altar

Gathering Collection Gift

Procession with Gifts

Preparation of and Prayer over the Gifts

[What's developing here is the practical aspect of getting the altar table ready for the Eucharistic Prayer; this is probably your busiest time because your function now is the practical one of helping to make all this happen.]

Liturgy of the Eucharist (Prayer)

Preface

Sanctus (Holy, holy, holy)

Words of Institution

Memorial Acclamation *(Christ has died. . . .)*

Memorial Prayers

Great Amen

A Place of Thanksgiving 53

[What's taking place now is the solemn memorial of our redemption; your part is to enter into the profound meaning of the Eucharistic Prayer.]

Communion Rites

    Lord's Prayer

    Sign of Peace

    Agnus Dei (Lamb of God)

    Procession to Communion

    Thanksgiving

    Prayer after Communion

[What's occurring here is the sharing in the Body and Blood of the Lord as a reconciled community; your task is to mirror the gestures and facilitate the movement of the assembly.]

Concluding Rite

    Final Blessing

    Dismissal

    Concluding Song and Recessional

[What's concluding now is our Sunday Eucharist, with a reminder that it continues through the coming week; your ministry is to help send your fellow parishioners off with a "Godspeed!"]

— Eight —
A PLACE OF AFFIRMATION

Psalm Passage

"I look to the faithful of the land; they alone can be my companions. Those who follow the way of integrity, they alone can enter my service."
(Ps 101:6)

Usher Story

IT felt kind of weird standing at the door and saying, "Hi," to my friends as they arrived for the evening youth Mass. But our youth minister had asked me and my boyfriend to think about being ushers and we said, "Hey, why not."

So we got trained and stuff and then were made part of the hospitality team at church.

Mary Leah—Windsor, Ontario

Reflection

There's something really affirming about being recognized, officially, by your parish community as a minister to that assembly. It further validates the fact that you have been open to deepen the call received at your Baptism to be another Christ.

So, here are two options for possible installation ceremonies that could be used in your parish, with any modifications, either within or outside of Mass.

OPTION A

Installation Service for Hospitality Ministers Outside of Mass

(The leader may be the bishop, pastor, deacon, or co-ordinator of Hospitality Team.)

GREETING

Leader:

Friends, the Lord is with us!

All: Amen!

PRAYER

Leader:

Gracious God, your love and compassion reaches out to all. Look upon us today as we rec-

A Place of Affirmation 57

ognize the men and women in our midst who have been called and formed by our parish community to serve as hospitality ministers. May their service as ushers and greeters remind us of our own responsibility to welcome and accompany one another in your Church.

All: Amen!

READING

Leader:
Let us be attentive to God's Holy Word.

Lector: Possible readings:

- 1 Corinthians 16:1-4. This is the passage about a collection taken up in the early Christian community.
- Hebrews 13:1-2. This is an exhortation regarding hospitality.
- James 2:1-4. This is a reminder about resisting favoritism toward certain members of the congregation.

Lector:
The Word of the Lord.

All: Thanks be to God.

RESPONSE

Left Side
I raise my eyes to the mountains. From where will my help come?

Right Side
My help comes from the Lord, the maker of heaven and earth.

Left Side
God will not allow your foot to slip; your guardian does not sleep.

Right Side
Truly, the guardian of Israel never slumbers nor sleeps.

Left Side
The Lord is your guardian; the Lord is your shade at your right hand.

Right Side
By day the sun cannot harm you, nor the moon by night.

Left Side
The Lord will guard you from all evil, will always guard your life.

A Place of Affirmation

Both Sides

The Lord will guard your coming and going both now and forever.

COMMISSIONING

(Here the Leader addresses the community with a few words about the ministry of hospitality.)

Leader:

At this time I invite all those who have been prepared and are willing to serve this local church as hospitality ministers to come forward.

(You may wish to have the hospitality ministers face the congregation as they respond.)

Leader:

Do you accept the ministry of hospitality to which you have been called?

Ushers/Greeters: I do.

Leader:

Do you promise to serve this parish community by being:

- a minister of welcome *(pause after each phrase)*
- a provider of comfort
- a messenger of respect

- a facilitator of participation
- an agent of safety
- a community animator

Ushers/Greeters: I do.

Leader:

On behalf of this parish community, I affirm your desire for service and commission you as a hospitality minister. (Here the leader may distribute a commissioning certificate or some other symbol of the ministry to each one. A sample certificate is on the next page.)

All: Thanks be to God. *(Applause is in order!)*

OPTION B:

Installation Service for Hospitality Ministers within Mass

The commissioning section of the preceding service may take place after the *Prayer After Communion* and before the *Final Blessing and Dismissal*. The newly commissioned hospitality ministers can then process out with the liturgical ministers and presider.

• **a messenger of respect** •

• **a community animator** •

The Community of _____
(Name of diocese or parish)

commissions _____

to serve our community of believers as

_____

"Do not neglect hospitality, for through it some have unknowingly entertained angels." **(Heb. 13:2)**

_____ _____
Date   *Signature*

• **a minister of welcome** •

• **a provider of comfort** •

• **an agent of safety** •

• **a facilitator of participation** •

THE JOY OF WORSHIPING TOGETHER
Father Rod Damico
". . . a much-needed volume about how and why we worship" —Fr. Paul Keenan
No. RP166/04   ISBN 1-878718-74-6 $5.95

THE JOY OF BEING AN ALTAR SERVER
Joseph M. Champlin
". . . a down-to-earth, hands-on resource for servers of any age."
—Msgr. Kevin Kostelnik
No. RP162/04   ISBN 1-878718-66-5 $5.95

THE JOY OF MUSIC MINISTRY
John Michael Talbot
"I encourage every pastor, musician, parish staff member, . . . to read this book."
—Fr. Dale Fushek
No. RP145/04   ISBN 1-878718-63-0 $6.95

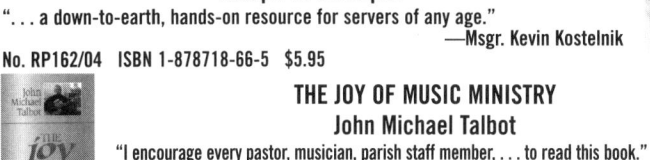

THE JOY OF BEING A LECTOR
Mitch Finley
". . . practical, full of useful suggestions on how to be a better lector."
—Fr. Joseph Champlin
No. RP123/04   ISBN 1-878718-57-6 $5.95
Also Available in Spanish: La Alegria De Ser Lector   No. RPS 123/04 $5.95

THE JOY OF BEING A CATECHIST
Gloria Durka, Ph.D.
"Chock-full of suggestions both practical and spiritual for gaining or maintaining our visions . . . perfect end-of-year gift." —Religion Teachers Journal
No. RP520/04   ISBN 1-878718-27-4 $4.95
Also Available in Spanish: La Alegria De Ser Catequista   RPS520/04 $4.95

THE JOY OF TEACHING
Joanmarie Smith, C.S.J.
". . . a lovely gift book for all proclaimers of the gospel." —Religion Teachers Journal
No. RP114/04   ISBN 1-878718-44-4 $5.95
Also Available in Spanish: La Alegria De Ser Educador—RPS114/04

THE JOY OF PREACHING
Fr. Rod Damico
"A gem . . . should be read by every deacon and candidate." —Deacon Jerry Wilson
No. RP142/04   ISBN 1-878718-61-4 $6.95

THE JOY OF BEING A EUCHARISTIC MINISTER
Mitch Finley
". . . provides insights meant to deepen one's relationship to the risen Christ."
—St. Anthony Messenger
No. RP010/04   ISBN 1-878718-45-2 $5.95
Also Available in Spanish: La Alegria De Ser Ministro De La Eucaristia—RPS010/04

www.catholicbookpublishing.com

Additional Titles Published by Resurrection Press, a Catholic Book Publishing Imprint

A Rachel Rosary *Larry Kupferman*	$4.50
Blessings All Around *Dolores Leckey*	$8.95
Catholic Is Wonderful *Mitch Finley*	$4.95
Come, Celebrate Jesus! *Francis X. Gaeta*	$4.95
Days of Intense Emotion *Keeler/Moses*	$12.95
Feasts of Life *Jim Vlaun*	$12.95
From Holy Hour to Happy Hour *Francis X. Gaeta*	$7.95
Grace Notes *Lorraine Murray*	$9.95
Healing through the Mass *Robert DeGrandis, SSJ*	$9.95
Our Grounds for Hope *Fulton J. Sheen*	$7.95
The Healing Rosary *Mike D.*	$5.95
Healing Your Grief *Ruthann Williams, OP*	$7.95
Life, Love and Laughter *Jim Vlaun*	$7.95
Living Each Day by the Power of Faith *Barbara Ryan*	$8.95
Loving Yourself for God's Sake *Adolfo Quezada*	$5.95
The Joy of Being an Altar Server *Joseph Champlin*	$5.95
The Joy of Being a Catechist *Gloria Durka*	$4.95
The Joy of Being a Eucharistic Minister *Mitch Finley*	$5.95
The Joy of Being a Lector *Mitch Finley*	$5.95
The Joy of Being an Usher *Gretchen Hailer, RSHM*	$5.95
The Joy of Marriage Preparation *McDonough/Marinelli*	$5.95
The Joy of Music Ministry *J.M. Talbot*	$6.95
The Joy of Preaching *Rod Damico*	$6.95
The Joy of Teaching *Joanmarie Smith*	$5.95
The Joy of Worshiping Together *Rod Damico*	$5.95
Lights in the Darkness *Ave Clark, O.P.*	$8.95
Meditations for Survivors of Suicide *Joni Woelfel*	$8.95
Mother Teresa *Eugene Palumbo, S.D.B.*	$5.95
Personally Speaking *Jim Lisante*	$8.95
Practicing the Prayer of Presence *Muto/van Kaam*	$8.95
Prayers from a Seasoned Heart *Joanne Decker*	$8.95
Praying the Lord's Prayer with Mary *Muto/van Kaam*	$8.95
Praying through Our Lifetraps *John Cecero, SJ*	$9.95
Rising from the Ashes *Adolfo Quezada*	$4.95
5-Minute Miracles *Linda Schubert*	$4.95
Season of New Beginnings *Mitch Finley*	$4.95
Season of Promises *Mitch Finley*	$4.95
St. Katharine Drexel *Daniel McSheffery*	$12.95
Stay with Us *John Mullin, SJ*	$3.95
Surprising Mary *Mitch Finley*	$7.95
What He Did for Love *Francis X. Gaeta*	$5.95
Woman Soul *Pat Duffy, OP*	$7.95
You Are My Beloved *Mitch Finley*	$10.95

For a free catalog call 1-800-892-6657
Visit our website: www.catholicbookpublishing.com